Musty-Crusty Animals 123

Lola M. Schaefer

Heinemann Library
Chicago, Illinois

© 2002 Reed Educational & Professional Publishing
Published by Heinemann Library,
an imprint of Reed Educational & Professional Publishing,
Chicago, Illinois

Customer Service 888-454-2279
Visit our website at www.heinemannlibrary.com

Designed by Sue Emerson/Heinemann Library and Ginkgo Creative, Inc.
Printed and bound in the U.S.A. by Lake Book

06 05 04 03 02
10 9 8 7 6 5 4 3 2 1

Library of Congress Cataloging-in-Publication Data
Schaefer, Lola M., 1950-
    Musty-crusty animals 123 / Lola Schaefer.
        p. cm. — (Musty-crusty animals)
Includes index.
Summary: A counting book featuring a variety of crustaceans.
    ISBN 1-58810-519-9 (lib. bdg.)   ISBN 1-58810-728-0 (pbk. bdg.)
    1. Counting—Juvenile literature. 2. Crustacea—Juvenile literature. 3. Sea horses—Juvenile literature.
    4. Limulus polyphemus—Juvenile literature. [1. Crustaceans. 2. Counting.] I. Title.
    QA113 .S378 2002
    513.2'11—dc21
    [[

                                    2001003288

Acknowledgments
The author and publishers are grateful to the following for permission to reproduce copyright material:
p. 3 E. R. Degginger/Color Pic, Inc.; p. 5 Jane Burton/Bruce Coleman Inc.; p. 7 David Liebman; p. 9 Gary Meszaros/Bruce Coleman Inc.; p. 11 Jeff Rotman Photography; p. 13 Doug Perrine/Jeff Rotman Photography; p. 15 David Wrobel/Visuals Unlimited; p. 17 Rudie Kuiter/Seapics.com; p. 19 William S. Ormerod, Jr./Visuals Unlimited; p. 21 H. W. Robinson/Visuals Unlimited; p. 22 Dwight Kuhn

Cover photographs courtesy of (L–R): John G. Shedd Aquarium/Visuals Unlimited; Jane Burton/Bruce Coleman Inc.; David Wrobel/Visuals Unlimited

Special thanks to our advisory panel for their help in the preparation of this book:

Eileen Day, Preschool Teacher
Chicago, IL

Paula Fischer, K–1 Teacher
Indianapolis, IN

Sandra Gilbert,
Library Media Specialist
Houston, TX

Angela Leeper,
Educational Consultant
North Carolina Department
of Public Instruction
Raleigh, NC

Pam McDonald, Reading Teacher
Winter Springs, FL

Melinda Murphy,
Library Media Specialist
Houston, TX

Helen Rosenberg, MLS
Chicago, IL

Anna Marie Varakin,
Reading Instructor
Western Maryland College

Special thanks to Dr. Randy Kochevar of the Monterey Bay Aquarium for his help in the preparation of this book.

Some words are shown in bold, **like this.**
You can find them in the picture glossary on page 23.

One 1

A horseshoe crab has one
long, pointed tail.

Two 2

Lobsters have two big **claws.**

The claws hold, tear, and cut fish or crabs.

Three 3

Three hermit crabs
eat **seaweed**.

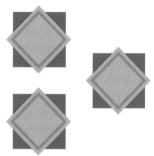

Four 4

Crayfish have four **antennae** on their heads.

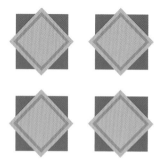

Five 5

Five young lobsters could fit inside your hand.

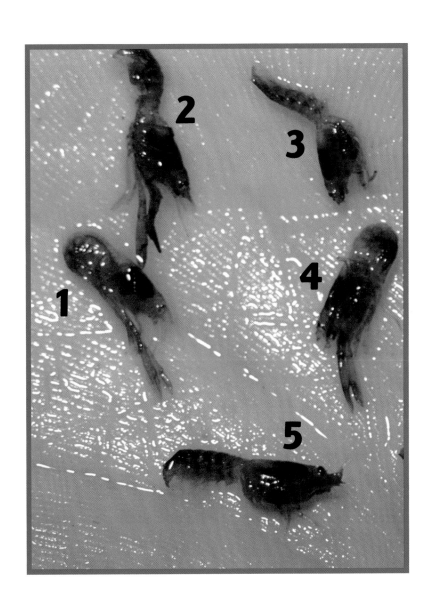

Six 6

Six lobsters crawl
on the ocean floor.

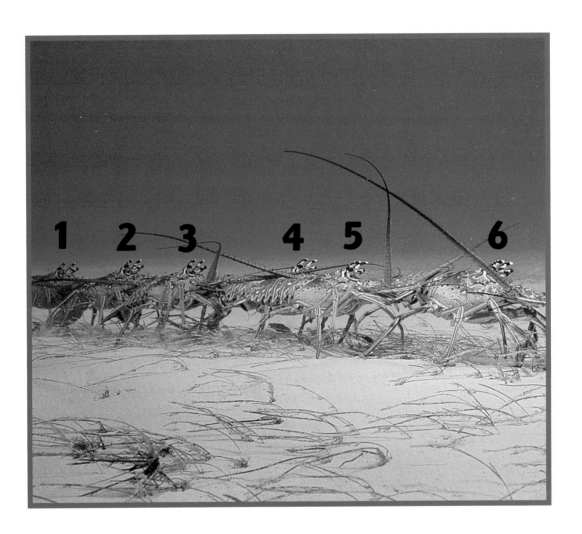

Seven 7

These seven hermit crabs all carry different shells on their backs.

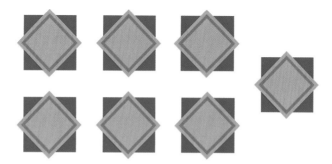

Eight   8

Eight young sea horses swim in the ocean.

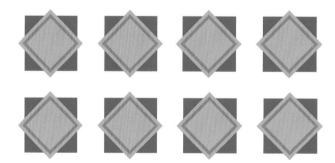

Nine   9

Nine barnacles wait for the next wave to bring them food.

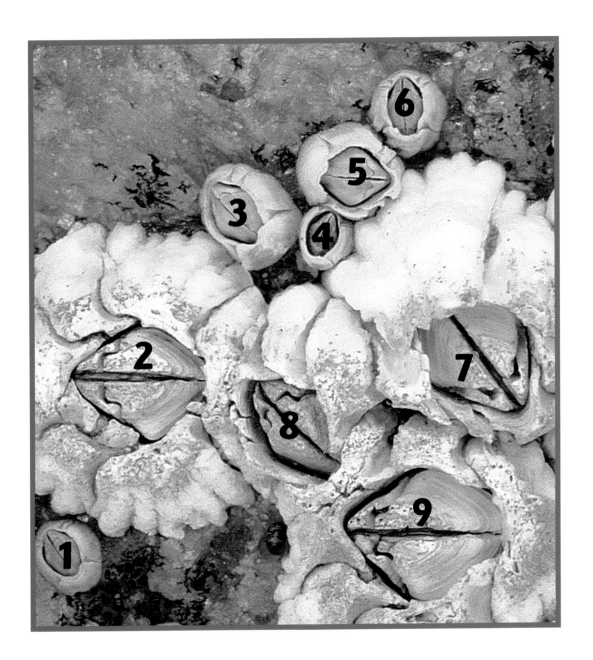

19

Ten 10

Crayfish have ten legs.

Two legs have **claws** and eight legs walk.

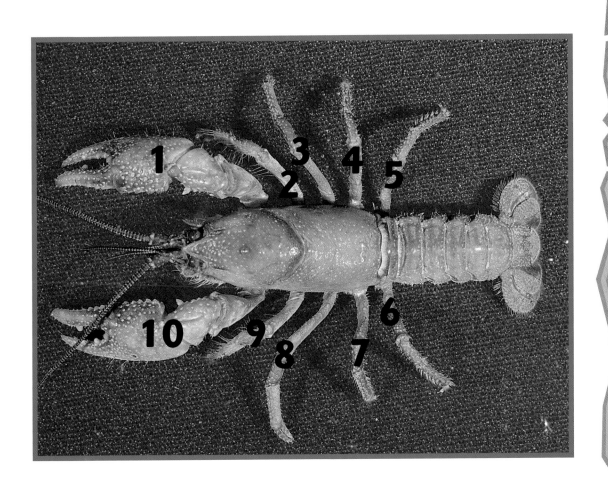

Look Closely!

How many horseshoe crabs can you count on the beach?

Look for the answer on page 24.

Picture Glossary

antennae
(an-TEN-ee)
pages 8–9

claw
pages 4–5, 20–21

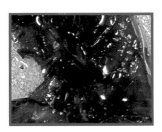

seaweed
pages 6–7

Note to Parents and Teachers

Using this book, children can practice basic mathematical skills while learning interesting facts about musty-crusty animals. Help children see the relationship between the numerals 1 through 10 and the block icons at the bottom of each text page. Extend the concept by drawing ten "blocks" on a sheet of construction paper. Cut out the paper "blocks." Together, read *Musty-Crusty Animals 123*, and as you do so, ask the child to place the appropriate number of "blocks" on the photograph. This activity can also be done using manipulatives such as dried beans or small plastic building blocks.

! CAUTION: Remind children that it is not a good idea to handle wild animals. Children should wash their hands with soap and water after they touch any animal.

Index

Answer to quiz on page 22
There are ten horseshoe crabs on the beach.